THE CIVIL WAR

SLAVERY & THE ABOLITION MOVEMENT

THE CIVIL WAR

SLAVERY & THE ABOLITION MOVEMENT

MASON CREST

Mason Crest
450 Parkway Drive, Suite D
Broomall, PA 19008
www.masoncrest.com

Cataloging-in-Publication Data on file with the Library of Congress.

Printed and bound in the United States of America.

First printing
9 8 7 6 5 4 3 2 1

ISBN: 978-1-4222-3883-7
Series ISBN: 978-1-4222-3881-3
ebook ISBN: 978-1-4222-7893-2
ebook series ISBN: 978-1-4222-7891-8

Produced by Regency House Publishing Limited
The Manor House
High Street
Buntingford
Hertfordshire
SG9 9AB
United Kingdom

www.regencyhousepublishing.com

Text copyright © 2018 Regency House Publishing Limited/Jonathan Sutherland and
Diane Canwell.

PAGE 2: Relaxed scene of soldiers from the Army of the Potomac eat their meal in the company of an African American, probably a "contraband," employed to cook and perform work for the soldiers. ca.1862–65.

PAGE 3: On April 19, 1866, African Americans staged a huge celebration of the fourth anniversary of the District of Columbia's Emancipation Act.

PAGE 5: Enslaved African American family representing five generations born on the plantation of J.J. Smith, Beaufort, South Carolina.

PAGE 6: Union army guard and other men in front of a building designated "Price, Birch & Co., Dealers in Slaves," in Alexandria, Virginia. ca. 1863.

TITLES IN THE CIVIL WAR SERIES:

The Origins of the Civil War
Slavery and the Abolition Movement
The Battle of Gettysburg – The Turning Point in the Civil War
The Politics of the Civil War
Civil War Victory and the Costly Aftermath

CONTENTS

Lincoln Memorial 10

Chapter One:
The Call for Abolition 14

Chapter Two:
Abolition Gains Pace 30

Chapter Three:
The Breakaway Begins 38

Time Line of the Civil War 68

Educational Videos 71

Examples of Confederate Uniforms 72

Examples of Union (Federal) Uniforms 74

Series Glossary of Key Terms 76

Further Reading and Internet Resources 77

Index 78

Further Information 80

KEY ICONS TO LOOK FOR:

Words to Understand: These words with their easy-to-understand definitions will increase the reader's understanding of the text, while building vocabulary skills.

Sidebars: This boxed material within the main text allows readers to build knowledge, gain insights, explore possibilities, and broaden their perspectives by weaving together additional information to provide realistic and holistic perspectives.

Educational Videos: Readers can view videos by scanning our QR codes, providing them with additional content to supplement the text. Examples include news coverage, moments in history, speeches, iconic sports moments, and much more!

Text-Dependent Questions: These questions send the reader back to the text for more careful attention to the evidence presented here.

Research Projects: Readers are pointed toward areas of further inquiry connected to each chapter. Suggestions are provided for projects that encourage deeper research and analysis.

Series Glossary of Key Terms: This back-of-the-book glossary contains terminology used throughout the series. Words found here increase the reader's ability to read and comprehend high-level books and articles in this field.

Abraham Lincoln.

Lincoln Memorial

The grand Lincoln Memorial is an American national monument built to honor the 16th President of the United States, Abraham Lincoln. It was designed by Henry Bacon, a New York architect. He had spent time studying in Europe where he was influenced and inspired by ancient Greek architecture. It was based on the architecture of a Greek temple. There are 36 Doric columns, each one representing one state of the U.S. at the date of President Lincoln's death.

The memorial contains a large seated sculpture of Abraham Lincoln. The nineteen-foot tall statue of Abraham Lincoln was designed by Daniel Chester French who was a leading sculptor from Massachusetts. The marble statue was carved in white Georgia marble by the Piccirilli brothers. The interior murals were painted by Jules Guerin. Ernest C. Bairstow created the exterior details with carvings by Evelyn Beatrice Longman. The memorial is inscribed with Lincoln's famous speech, "The Gettysburg Address." The words of the speech are etched into the wall to inspire all Americans just as it did in 1863. To the right is the entire Second Inaugural Address, given by Lincoln in March 1865. The memorial itself is 190 feet long, 119 feet wide, and almost 100 feet high. It took 8 years to complete from 1914–1922.

At its most basic level the Lincoln Memorial symbolizes the idea of Freedom. The Lincoln Memorial is often used as a gathering place for protests and political rallies. The Memorial has become a symbolically sacred venue especially for the Civil Rights movement. On August 28, 1963, the memorial grounds were the site of the *March on Washington for Jobs and Freedom*, which proved to the high point of the *American Civil Rights Movement*. It is estimated that approximately 250,000 people came to the event, where they heard Martin Luther King, Jr. deliver his historic speech *"I have a Dream."* King's speech, with its language of patriotism and its evocation of Lincoln's Gettysburg Address, was meant to match the symbolism of the Lincoln Memorial as a monument to national unity.

The Lincoln Memorial is located on the western end of the National Mall in Washington, D.C., across from the Washington Monument, and towers over the Reflecting Pool. The memorial is maintained by the U.S. National Park Service, and receives approximately 8 million visitors each year. It is open 24 hours a day and is free to all visitors.

LEFT: Group of slaves on J.J. Smith's plantation in Beaufort, South Carolina, liberated after Union forces captured Beaufort and surrounding areas in late 1861. Photograph by Timothy O'Sullivan.

Chapter One
THE CALL FOR ABOLITION

On Saturday January 1, 1831, the first issue of *The Liberator* was published in Boston, Massachusetts. This was a pro-abolitionist newspaper published by William Lloyd Garrison and Isaac Knapp. In the first issue, Garrison wrote: "Urge we not to use moderation in a cause like the present. I am in earnest – I will not equivocate – I will not excuse – I will not retreat a single inch – AND I WILL BE HEARD. The apathy of the people is enough to make every statue leap from its pedestal, and to hasten the resurrection of the dead."

Words to Understand

Abolitionist: A person with the principle of fostering abolition, especially slavery.

Fugitive: Running away to avoid being captured.

Quaker: A member of the Religious Society of Friends, a Christian sect founded by George Fox ca.1650.

Garrison was preaching to the converted. His tiny readership consisted of either African-Americans in the North or fellow white **abolitionists**. But he persisted, hoping to bring his views to a wider audience. As the word spread, Southerners began to fear slave revolts and more people became convinced that slavery needed to be abolished. Garrison was

LEFT: Slaves working at an early cotton gin.

OPPOSITE: In 1864 George N. Barnard was made the official photographer for the United States Army, Chief Engineer's Office, Division of the Mississippi. He followed Union General William T. Sherman's infamous March to the Sea and in 1866 published an album of 61 photographs, "Photographic Views of Sherman's Campaign." This is a photograph taken in Whitehall Street, Atlanta, Georgia, shortly after Sherman had taken the city in 1864.

LEFT: Idealized view of a cotton plantation on the Mississippi River, evocative of the Southern antebellum era of pre-Civil War prosperity and slavery. Color lithograph, 1884.

not the first to believe that slavery had no place in a Christian society.

Back in 1746 a **Quaker**, John Woolman, visited the Southern states and saw his fellow Quakers using slaves. Deeply troubled by what he had seen, he convinced the Society of Friends to publish a statement in favor of emancipation and in 1754 published his own views on slavery in *Some Considerations on the Keeping of Negroes*. Quakers soon became some of the most vociferous critics of slavery and many more wrote pamphlets condemning the practice.

But Quakers were not the only religious group to consider slavery a sin. In 1780 the Methodists also came out against slavery, a handful of them having already freed their slaves; five years later, Methodists still holding slaves would be excommunicated.

By the end of the 18th century, Congregationalists, Baptists and Presbyterians had joined the Quakers and Methodists in their condemnation of slavery. All made statements against slavery, and urged their members to free their slaves and take up active roles in anti-slavery societies. There were also early attempts to phase out slavery gradually rather than immediately. The Presbyterian clergyman, David Rice, from Kentucky, proposed that states should import no more slaves, free those born after 1792 and then gradually free the rest. His published view, *Slavery Inconsistent with Justice and Good Policy*, also played on the notion that

WILLIAM LLOYD GARRISON (1805–1879)

William Lloyd Garrison was born on December 10, 1805. He was the son of a merchant sailor in Newburyport, Massachusetts. Later, he became a prominent American abolitionist, journalist, and social crusader. In 1831 he founded with Isaac Knapp, the abolitionist newspaper *The Liberator*.

It was published in Massachusetts until slavery was abolished after the Civil War.

When he was 25, Garrison joined the antislavery movement, later crediting the 1826 book of Presbyterian Reverend John Rankin of Ohio, *Letters on Slavery*, for attracting him to the cause. For a brief time he became associated with the American Colonization Society, an organization that promoted the resettlement of free blacks to Liberia on the west coast of Africa. Eventually Garrison rejected colonization and publicly apologized for his mistake. Fortunately William Lloyd Garrison lived long enough to see the Union break apart under the weight of slavery and he also survived to see Abraham Lincoln issue the Emancipation Proclamation during the Civil War and then thirty-four years after publishing *The Liberator*, Garrison saw the Thirteenth Amendment to the Consitution go into effect, banning slavery for ever.

In the last year of his life, Garrison, suffering from kidney disease went to live with his daughter Fanny, in New York City. He died on May 24, 1879. He was buried in Forest Hills Cemetery in Jamaica Plain, Massachusetts on May 28. Flags were flown at half-staff across Boston, Massachusetts.

ideals were put into practice, in that while the British were held to be denying Americans the right to direct their own affairs, the Americans

an enslaved body of people was always a threat to the Republic, and could be expected to rise up one day and overthrow the state.

The great paradox of slavery lay at the very heart of the American Revolution and the Declaration of Independence. When Thomas Jefferson wrote the first draft, his intention was to condemn slavery. He blamed the English, and principally George III, who had vetoed laws passed by the state of Virginia against the importation of slaves.

The declaration enshrined the noble ideals of universal equality and basic human rights. But there was a huge inconsistency in the way these

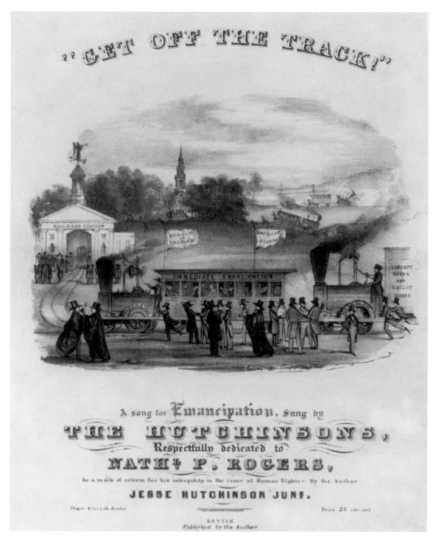

OPPOSITE ABOVE:
Pioneers of Freedom
features individual portraits of Charles Sumner, Henry Ward Beecher, Wendell Phillips, William Lloyd Garrison, Gerrit Smith, Horace Greeley, and Henry Wilson. ca. 1866.

OPPOSITE BELOW: **The Sale**
A card painted by Henry Louis Stephens of an African-American slave being sold. ca. 1863.

LEFT: "Get off the Track!" A song for emancipation, composed by Jesse Hutchinson, Jr. The song was dedicated to the anti-slavery editor Nathanial Peabody Rogers.

ABOVE: The Parting – Buy us Too
A Card also by Henry Louis Stephens, showing an African-American slave being separated from his family. ca. 1863.

themselves were guilty of enslavement of another kind. Once recognized as such, the inconsistency could only find a remedy in the spread and implementation of anti-slavery beliefs.

This, however, was a slow process. The Continental Congress, during the revolutionary war itself, banned the importation of slaves in 1774, and in the North, where slavery had never been as widespread, abolition slowly took effect over the next three decades. Vermont and New Hampshire led the

way and Rhode Island and Connecticut followed in 1784. Pennsylvania abolished slavery in 1780 but found constant policing was required to stamp it out, while Massachusetts, with a slave population of three percent, made the practice illegal in 1790. It took until 1799 to pass the necessary legislation in New York, however, and New Jersey followed suit in 1804. Both of these states had a slave population of between eight and 12 percent.

THE ABOLITION CATASTROPHE,
Or the November Smash-up.

ABOVE: Lincoln's support of abolition is portrayed here as a liability in his race to the White House against Democratic candidate George B. McClellan. At top a smoothly run train "Union" heads straight for the White House. The engine is labeled "Democracy" and the first car, in which McClellan stands in the role of engineer, flies a flag "Constitution." The other cars are labeled "Union" and are occupied by happy, cheering Democrats. McClellan taunts, "Wouldn't you like to swap horses now? Lincoln?" (probably a reference to Lincoln's replacement of him as commander of the Army of the

Potomac). Several of his passengers comment on the wreck of the Republican train below.

But this did not make all slaves free: there was the question of reimbursing the slave-owners. To avoid this, slaves got their freedom after a period of time had elapsed, and some had to wait for nearly 30 years.

Despite the progress made in the North, slave-owners themselves held the balance of power in the South,

and simply ignored the abolitionists. Thomas Jefferson led the movement to prevent slavery from establishing itself in the Western territories when the North-West Ordnance was passed in 1787, and he was instrumental in ensuring the foreign trade in slaves was brought to an end, it being officially outlawed on January 1, 1808.

Having "defeated" slavery in the North, the abolitionist movement began to lose its way in the 1820s, being content to approach the issue by tackling it in small, measured steps. Churches still existed that advocated

HARRIET TUBMAN
(Ca. 1822–1913)

Harriet Tubman, born Araminta "Minty" Ross was an American abolitionist and humanitarian. She was also an armed scout and spy for the United States Army during the American Civil War. Born into slavery in the plantation of Edward Brodess in Dorcester County, Maryland, Tubman escaped to Philadelpia in 1849, and subsequently made multiple missions to rescue approximately seventy enslaved families and friends, using the network of anti-slavery activists and secret safe houses known as the Underground Railroad. Known as the "Moses of her people," she later helped abolitionist John Brown recruit men for his raid on Harpers Ferry, and in the post-war era was an active participant in the struggle for women's suffrage.

During the Civil War, Tubman worked for the Union army, first as a cook and nurse, and then as an armed scout and spy. She lead an armed expedition in the war and she guided the raid at Combahee Ferry, which liberated more than 700 slaves. After the war, she retired to the family home at a property she had purchased in 1859 in Auburn, New York, where she cared for her aging and frail parents. She was active in the women's suffrage movement until illness overtook her and she had to be admitted to a home for elderly African Americans that she had helped to establish years earlier. After she died in 1913, she became an icon of American courage and freedom.

excommunication for slave-owners, but others repealed or simply ignored the requirement not to hold slaves. Although it was generally believed that the moral cause had been won, it was also believed that slave-owners would come around to a similar way of thinking given time.

An odd mix of abolitionists, politicians, and slave-owners set up the American Colonization Society in 1816. They proposed to give slaves the

ABOVE: Am I not a Man and a Brother?
Woodcut.
An illustration for John Greenleaf Whittier's poem, "Our Countrymen in Chains," of 1837. The design was originally the seal of the Society for the Abolition of Slavery in England in the 1780s, and appeared on medallions made for the society by Josiah Wedgwood.

RIGHT: John Quincy Adams (1767–1848), was president from 1825–1829. After his presidency he was elected to the House of Representatives. He is most famous for his formation of the Monroe Doctrine.

ABOLITION OF THE SLAVE TRADE, OR THE MAN THE MASTER.

ABOVE: Abolition of the Slave Trade or The Man, the Master
A British print showing the roles of slave and master reversed, 1789.

opportunity to set up a Christian state in West Africa. Called Liberia, the new republic would prove that a slave, once freed, could be as civilized as any white person. But it is clear that others saw this as a means of ridding the United States of its ex-slaves once and for all.

Congress passed the first Fugitive Slave Act in 1793. This made it dangerous to help runaway slaves, though many continued to do so all the same. An even more draconian act was passed in 1850, making those aiding and abetting the escape of a slave subject to a $1,000 fine. Runaway slaves escaping from the South rarely lingered in the Northern states, especially if they lacked the necessary documents proving they were free. The first safe destination, being slave-free, was therefore Canada, whence a sea passage could be taken to the West Indies.

During this period, an active minority was directly involved in helping as many abolitionists, Quakers, and freed and fugitive slaves fleeing bounty hunters, as possible, the Rev. John Rankin, of Ripley, Ohio, being one of these. His organization, known as the Underground Railroad,

provided a network of guides and safe houses stretching from the South to the Northern states and beyond.

It is not known how many were saved by the actions of the Underground Railroad, though estimates range between 25 and 100,000. Whatever the figure, it was a drop in the ocean, and most slaves would have had to wait for the Union army to free them or until the Civil War had been won.

Although Rankin is credited with setting up a loose network of escape roots, others made even greater efforts. Foremost among these was Harriet Tubman, herself an escaped slave from Maryland, who became the "Moses" of her people and guided thousands to safety both before and during the Civil War. Others include Livi Coffin and Isaac Hopper, while Thomas Garrett is credited with assisting 3,000 **fugitive** slaves.

Slaves had been attending Evangelical Christian Churches, led by white missionaries and supported by benevolent societies, since the 1790s. Gradually, however, their own African Methodist Episcopal Church was established. Its first bishop was

OPPOSITE: Distinguished Colored Men
First published ca. 1883 by A. Muller & Co. It features Frederick Douglass, Robert Brown Elliott, Blanche K. Bruce, William Wells Brown, Prof. R.T. Greener, Rt. Rev. Richard Allen, J.H. Rainey, E.D. Basset, John Mercer Langston, P.B.S. Pinchback, and Henry Highland Garnet.

RIGHT: James Birney became secretary of the American Anti-slavery Society in 1837.

Richard Allen, who led attacks on the American Colonization Society and helped to found a Negro Convention Movement.

By the time Garrison published his *Liberator* in 1831, the majority of his readership was black. Printing presses spread political thought to the far-flung corners of the United States, and abolitionists would use this revolution in communications to give fresh life to their cause. Garrison found a willing partner in Benjamin Lundy – a Quaker who had sold his saddle-making business to found his own antislavery newspaper, *The*

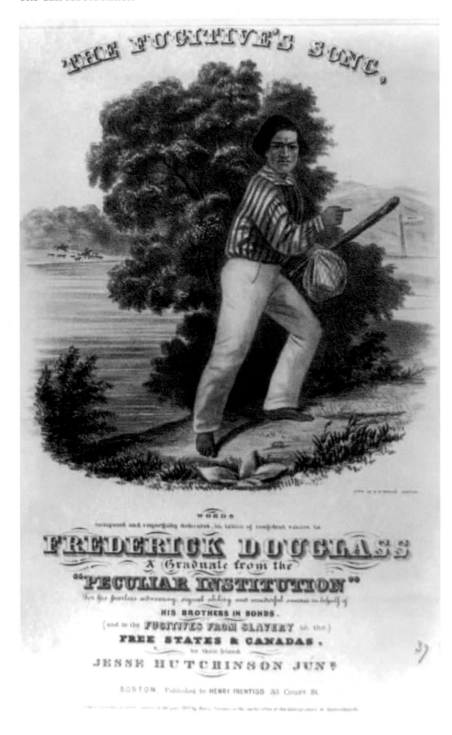

Genius of Universal Emancipation, first published in 1821. Lundy managed to limp along financially, at the same time publicizing the Convention for Promoting the Abolition of Slavery among other abolitionist groups.

The two had collaborated with one another for a short time after they met in 1828. But Lundy supported colonizing Mexico with freed slaves, while Garrison was against colonization and wished to see an outright end to slavery. Garrison published his arguments in 1832 in *Thoughts on African Colonization*, in which he roundly attacked all factions of the American Colonization

Society and called for immediate emancipation. He strongly believed that slave-owners would never relinquish their slaves until they accepted it as sinful to hold another man in bondage.

In many ways Garrison echoed the views of British abolitionists, who had effected the end of slavery in the West Indies, where they had won the moral argument. In his discussions with Northern blacks it had become clear to Garrison that almost all of them were against colonization. It was also obvious that they despised slave-owners and believed them undeserving of a voice in the debate.

Meanwhile, Arthur and Lewis Tappan, wealthy New York merchants implacably opposed to slavery, called a meeting in 1831. The outcome was the creation of the New England Anti-Slavery Society, and its members were heavily influenced by Garrison's anti-colonization views and even more so by the British government, when it abolished slavery in 1833.

The New England group now sought to spread its views across the

OPPOSITE LEFT: The Fugitive's Song
Lithograph, 1845.
Sheet music illustrated with a portrait of the prominent black abolitionist, Frederick Douglass, in the guise of a runaway slave.

OPPOSITE RIGHT: Arthur Tappan 1786–1865) was an American abolitionist. He was born in Northampton, Massachusetts to a Calvinist family.

FREDERICK DOUGLASS (1818–1895)

Frederick Douglass was an African-American social reformer, abolitionist, orator, author, and statesman. Following his escape at the age of 20 from slavery in Maryland, he became a national leader of the abolitionist movement in Massachusetts and New York. He was renowned for his oratory and incisive anti-slavery writings. He made thousands of powerful speeches and persuasive editorials against slavery and racism. As the Civil War progressed and emancipation seemed more imminent, Douglass continued tirelessly to fight for equal rights and citizenship throughout his life.

Research Projects

In 1746, Quaker, John Woolman was greatly troubled when he saw his fellow Quakers using slaves. Summarize his early life, education, career, anti-slavery activities, and final days.

nation. On December 4, 1833, 63 people met in Philadelphia to establish the American Anti-Slavery Society. Significantly, three of the delegates were black men and four were white women.

They were all Evangelical Christians, Protestants with strong moral principles. Their focus was the Declaration of Independence, which says that "all men are created equal." In the South this was still clearly not the case, and they advocated immediate emancipation without compensation. This was a radical departure, rather than a mainstream view, and could easily have floundered at its inception. Four years later, however, New York had 274 such societies, Massachusetts 145 and Ohio 213. By 1838 there were 250,000 members in 1,350 societies. To spread the word and arrange the establishment of new societies, the group had over 60 agents on the road, all of whom espoused immediate emancipation.

THE RESURRECTION OF HENRY BOX BROWN AT PHILADELPHIA

OPPOSITE: The resurrection of Henry Box Brown, who escaped from Richmond, Virginia, in a box. Here, he emerges from the box in the office of Pennsylvania's Anti-Slavery Society. Present is Frederick Douglass (left) holding a claw hammer.

RIGHT: Joshua R. Giddings (1795–1864). The representative for Ohio, he resigned in 1842 after a vote of censure had been passed on him because of his defense of the slave mutineers in the Creole case, which caused tensions between the U.S. and Britain. In 1841, a brig named the Creole was transporting 135 slaves between Hampton Roads and New Orleans, when 19 of them revolted, redirecting the ship to Nassau in the Bahamas, which was then a British colony.

Pamphlets and journals supported the work of the agents. The national society, in 1838, produced a staggering 647,000 copies of various papers, tracts, and pamphlets, while *The Liberator* had been joined by up to 40 other newspapers.

The movement used a petition system to encourage members. The names of those who signed the petition were published; politicians could see the names of voters on the lists and those who had not yet signed saw that the House of Representatives was being bombarded with abolitionist demands.

During the period 1837 to 1838, Congress received petitions bearing 414,000 signatures. The language of the petitions was designed to be provocative: slavery was described as a crime, one that corrupted the American way of life and which it was cowardice to ignore.

Text-Dependent Questions

1. Who was William Lloyd Garrison?

2. Name two religious groups who came out against slavery?

3. What was the American Colonization Society?

Chapter Two
ABOLITION GAINS PACE

The abolitionists tried to force religious bodies and reform societies to adopt an anti-slavery stance, and every success further promoted their cause. Each time one refused, however, they were bombarded with accusations of **hypocrisy** or cowardice, which caused enormous rifts within the churches. The Presbyterian Church split in 1837, the Methodist Episcopal Church in both 1842 and 1844, and the Baptists in 1845. In most cases the split followed a North-South divide.

But the abolitionists did not have it all their own way. In 1832 the Connecticut state legislature blocked the establishment of a mixed-race girls' school in Canterbury, leading to the arrest of the Quaker teacher, Prudence Crandall.

Meanwhile, the South refused to take this lying down; it was affronted by the attacks of the abolitionists. Georgia, for example, put a price of $5,000 on the head of Garrison, as a fugitive from justice, while Louisiana placed a price of $50,000 on Arthur Tappan. Southern politicians begged their Northern counterparts to do something to stop publication and distribution of what they saw as incendiary material, their fear being that the writings and actions of the abolitionists would encourage a slave rebellion. The South effectively tried to ban written or spoken abolitionist

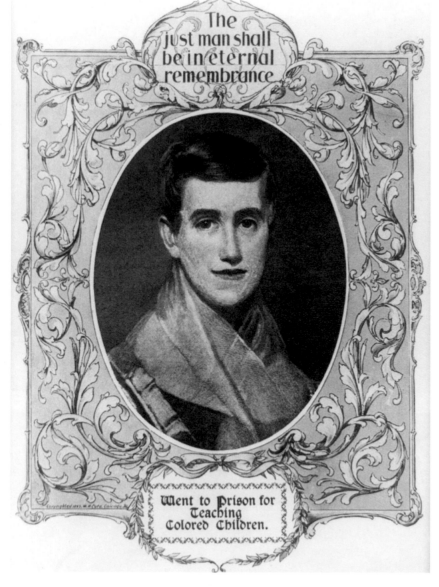

The just man shall be in eternal remembrance

Went to Prison for Teaching Colored Children.

LEFT: Prudence Crandall (1803–1890) was an American Quaker and teacher who was arrested and jailed for teaching African-American children.

OPPOSITE: Celebration of the Abolition of Slavery in the District of Columbia by the Colored People, Washington, April, 19 1866
Wood engraving by Frederick Dielman.

beliefs, imprisoning some, firing others, and whipping a few when they were caught.

There had been an attempt to ignore the abolitionist petitions in 1834. The senate had been having long and involved discussions on the subject of slavery, while former President John Quincy Adams of Massachusetts led attacks against the "gag rule," which ignored the petitions, seeing them as a threat to American liberty. The Southerners

Words to Understand

Hypocrisy: Behavior that does not agree with what a person claims or feels.

Methodist: A member of an evangelical Protestent chuch based on Wesleyan principles.

Prejudice: An unfair dislike of a person or group of because of race, sex, religion, etc.

Elijah Parish Lovejoy Was Killed By a Pro-slavery Mob November 7, 1837

On November 7, 1837, Elijah Parish Lovejoy was killed by a pro-slavery mob while defending the site of his anti-slavery newspaper, *The Saint Louis Observer*. His death deeply affected many Northerners and greatly strengthened the abolitionist (anti-slavery) cause.

were forced to defend every criticism of slavery, which ultimately led to a tailing-off of Northern sympathy. The gag rule was finally lifted in 1845.

There were as many as 165 anti-abolitionist riots in the period 1833 to 1838, some violent, others in the form of heckling or throwing rotten eggs. Abolitionists' homes were attacked, presses were destroyed and individuals beaten up.

James Birney was forced out of Kentucky in the 1830s and made for Cincinnati, desperate to see his anti-slavery newspaper, the *Philanthropist*, published. Despite warnings from abolitionists he went ahead and on July 30, 1836 the printing presses were destroyed by a mob. Garrison was attacked in Boston in October 1835 and Elijah Lovejoy was murdered in Illinois in 1837. Lovejoy had fled Missouri and moved to Alton, Illinois, where his presses had been wrecked on three occasions. When the mob attacked a fourth time, his warehouse was burned down, his press was thrown into the Ohio river and Lovejoy was shot five times.

The South had been forced to make compromises in the past, but now there was nothing that could satisfy its opponents. This was because the call for abolition had not come from the established politicians, with whom the South could have debated and brought about a mutually acceptable outcome. The abolitionists were outside this world; they were

OPPOSITE: Abolitionist James Birney. By Asa Park (1790-1827) in 1818.

RIGHT: Slave auction block at Green Hill Plantation, Virginia.

Research Projects

Elijah Parish Lovejoy (1802– 1837) was an American Presbyterian minister who was murdered by a pro-slavery mob. Summarize his early life, career, anti-slavery activities, and how he died.

aspiring politicians, community leaders and worse, educated blacks, with whom the South had no hope of ever reaching a compromise.

Direct, aggressive action to silence abolitionists did not work either. In murdering Lovejoy, the abolitionists had been handed a martyr on a plate. In fact, the North formed four abolitionist groups. First there were the radicals, typified by Garrison and Wendell Phillips, who were not only opposed to slavery, but to various institutions and values that allowed it to exist. The second group were the Ecclesiasticals, such as the **Methodist**, Orange Scott, who constantly criticized slavery and promoted a strong distaste for pro-slavery principles. The third group were the political abolitionists, Birney being a leading example, who was nominated for president at the Liberty Party convention in New York in

1840. The party believed that existing parties were too wedded to the slave-owners to ever press for abolition. Birney lost heavily in the 1840 presidential election and faired little better four years later.

The final group were the black abolitionists, some of whom also belonged to the other three groups. A network of black organizations had sprung up and their key role was to shame their white colleagues into pushing harder, using the black abolitionists' personal experiences of slavery and racial **prejudice**. Frederick Douglass was perhaps the best-known former slave, who had established strong political connections and lectured widely. He published an influential newspaper (first called the *North Star* and later *Frederick Douglass's Paper*) between 1847 and 1860.

The issue of slavery had been moving in and out of national politics ever since the American Revolution, gradually becoming a dominant issue, but deadlock and crisis were hanging in the air as the United States entered the 1850s. Northern radicals, like

Abraham Lincoln of Illinois and Joshua Giddings, were pressing for abolition in the District of Columbia, while, as yet, nothing had been decided about the new territories of California and New Mexico, which had gone to the U.S. folowing the Mexican War.

Meanwhile, the comparative power of North and South was still shifting in favor of the North and policy against the interests of the South was still being made.

EMANCIPATION OF THE SLAVES,
Proclamed on the 22d September 1862, by ABRAHAM LINCOLN, President of the United States of North America.
Published by J. Waeschle, Nº 162, North Third Sº Philadª

OPPOSITE: Emancipation Ordinance of Missouri
A splendid, large allegorical print commemorating the ordinance providing for the immediate emancipation of slaves in Missouri. The ordinance was passed on January 11, 1865, three weeks before the Thirteenth Amendment to the U.S. Constitution was proposed by Congress.

RIGHT: Emancipation of the slaves, proclamed [i.e. proclaimed] on the September 22, 1862, by Abraham Lincoln, President of the United States.

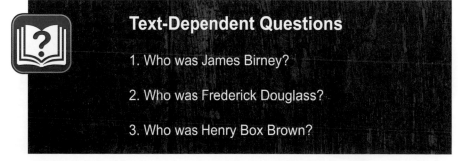

Text-Dependent Questions

1. Who was James Birney?

2. Who was Frederick Douglass?

3. Who was Henry Box Brown?

Chapter Three
THE BREAKAWAY BEGINS

The year 1850 saw a large number of major issues still waiting to be resolved and for a time the **dissolution** of the Union seemed to be the only way forward. The exact nature of the territories taken from the Mexicans needed careful thought, the debt and size of Texas required consideration, and there was the problem of slaves being sold in sight of the capitol in the District of Columbia and the increasing numbers of fugitive slaves. The result was the Missouri Compromise of 1850.

California would be admitted into the Union as a free state and the question of slavery in Utah and New Mexico would be left to the electorate. The Federal government would

Words to Understand

Citizen: A person who legally belongs to a country and has rights and protection of that country.

Dissolution: The process of making something end slowly or disappear.

Unconstitutional: Not allowed by the constitution of a country or government.

NOW READY:
THE
Dred Scott Decision.

OPINION OF CHIEF-JUSTICE
ROGER B. TANEY,
WITH AN INTRODUCTION,
BY DR. J. H. VAN EVRIE.
ALSO,
AN APPENDIX,
BY SAM. A. CARTWRIGHT, M.D., of New Orleans,
ENTITLED,
"Natural History of the Prognathous
Race of Mankind."
ORIGINALLY WRITTEN FOR THE NEW YORK DAY-BOOK.

THE GREAT WANT OF A BRIEF PAMPHLET, containing the famous decision of Chief-Justice Taney, in the celebrated Dred Scott Case, has induced the Publishers of the DAY-BOOK to present this edition to the public. It contains a Historical Introduction by Dr. Van Evrie, author of "Negroes and Negro Slavery," and an Appendix by Dr. Cartwright, of New Orleans, in which the physical differences between the negro and the white races are forcibly presented. As a whole, this pamphlet gives the *historical*, *legal*, and *physical* aspects of the "Slavery" Question in a concise compass, and should be circulated by thousands before the next presidential election. All who desire to answer the arguments of the abolitionists should read it. In order to place it before the masses, and induce Democratic Clubs, Democratic Town Committees, and all interested in the cause, to order it for distribution, it has been put down at the following low rates, for which it will be sent, free of postage, to any part of the United States. Dealers supplied at the same rate.

shoulder the debts of the former independent Texas and slavery would continue in the District of Columbia, but there would be an end to the slave trade. The main objection was the newly proposed Fugitive Slave Act. Northerners refused to exact the requirements of the law: heavy fines

OPPOSITE LEFT: Kentucky Senator Henry Clay.

OPPOSITE RIGHT: Dred Scott, the slave of an itinerant doctor-soldier, lost his case to obtain his freedom in 1857, after a High Court ruling that he had no right to plead his case; this was because he was black, and therefore not a citizen.

ABOVE: Newspaper article about the Dred Scott case.

JOHN BROWN (1800–1859)

John Brown was an American radical abolitionist who believed in the violent overthrow of the slavery in the United States. He was born in Torrington, Connecticut where he mingled with opponents of slavery. Despite documented business failures, Brown nonetheless deepened his ethics in fighting slavery. During the Bleeding Kansas Crisis, Brown, along with his sons, led small armed groups to attack pro-slavery settlers. In the eyes of Northern extremists Brown was quick to exploit his growing reputation. This crusade ended in his execution at Harper's Ferry in 1859. Brown was captured during the raid and later hanged. Experts in Civil War matters now conclude that the raid at Harper's Ferry did much to hasten the coming of the Civil War.

LEFT: John Brown and others inside the engine house of the Harper's Ferry Armory just before the U.S. Marines ram through the door.

ABOVE: The burning of the U.S. Arsenal at Harper's Ferry, April 18, 1861
Engraving by David Hunter Strother.

LEFT: The ruins of the Federal arsenal at Harper's Ferry, eventually destroyed in 1861, despite John Brown's earlier abortive attempts on it in 1859.

OPPOSITE: Photograph showing ruins of the armory at Harper's Ferry, West Virginia, at the confluence of the Shenandoah and Potomac rivers.

OVERLEAF: Photograph of Harper's Ferry, West Virginia, as it appears today.

for those who helped slaves and the denial of the fugitive's right to a trial. The South, however, was unwilling to accept any of the compromises unless the North complied. Southern elections in 1850 and 1851 heavily supported pro-compromise candidates, consequently the compromises set out by Henry Clay of Kentucky were more or less agreed.

There are several examples of Northerners defying the Fugitive Slave Act, as in the case of the slave, Shadrach (Boston, February 1, 1851). In each case, mobs of abolitionists worked to ensure that slaves remained free and were spirited out of the country.

By 1854 it seemed as though the pro-slavery lobby was winning the war of words and deeds, when the states of Nebraska and Kansas came up for debate. The result, after much political wrangling, was that the two states should be allowed to choose whether they adopted slavery or not. More seriously, Southerners were behind the proposed purchase or seizure of Cuba from the Spanish; this, too, was to be a slave state, but in the end nothing came of the plan.

Settlers from the Eastern states were flowing into Kansas, as were even more from the South, and it was to become the fighting ground of the pro-slavery factions against the abolitionists. The "free-state" settlers received harassment from the South, intent on making Kansas a slave state. Militant free-staters, like John Brown, called for men and weapons to protect the state of Kansas, where a civil war was all too likely; in the spring of 1856 a pro-slavery mob attacked the free-state town of Lawrence and sacked it. John Brown, in response, attacked the pro-slavery settlers in Pottawotomie, and the pro-slavers then plundered southern Kansas, where Brown lived. The fighting continued well into the summer of 1856.

President Buchanan came to power in 1856, promising to settle the slave question once and for all, and hoping to obtain a speedy resolution

OPPOSITE: James Buchanan (1791–1868) was the 15th president of the United States, from 1856–61.

RIGHT: Stephen A. Douglas was responsible for the highly controversial Kansas-Nebraska Act of 1854 that revived the issue of slavery.

to the Kansas civil war. Just two days after Buchanan's inaugural speech, the Supreme Court passed a judgement on the Dred Scott case, the results of which were to have long-lasting and dangerous implications. Dred Scott was the slave of a doctor who had joined the army in 1834. Posted to Illinois and then to Wisconsin, Scott had lived for 24 years in states where there was no slavery. Consequently, Scott's case hinged on these facts when he sued for freedom after his owner died. The Lower Missouri court found in Scott's favor, but the State Supreme Court found against him. He contested the case in the Federal District Court and then the Supreme Court. The Supreme Court ruled that a slave was not a **citizen**. Scott had been a slave in a slave state when the action had been brought, making the four years out of Missouri irrelevant. In short, Congress could not deprive a citizen of his property without due process of law. In effect, the court declared the Missouri Compromise **unconstitutional**.

Abraham Lincoln was nominated as the Republican candidate for

LEFT: John C. Breckinridge (1821–85), the 14th Vice President of the United States from 1857–61, under Buchanan, and a Confederate general.

OPPOSITE ABOVE: The Old State Capitol, Springfield, Illinois where Lincoln made his famous "House Divided" speech.

OPPOSITE BELOW: Abraham Lincoln by George Peter Alexander Healy, 1860. Philanthropist Thomas B. Bryan commissioned this portrait of the President-elect Lincoln.

An excerpt from Abraham Lincoln's "House Divided Speech"

"A house divided against itself cannot stand."

I believe this government cannot endure, permanently, half slave and half free.

I do not expect the Union to be dissolved – I do not expect the house to fall – but I do expect it will cease to be divided.

It will become all one thing or all the other.

Either the opponents of slavery, will arrest the further spread of it, and place it where the public mind shall rest in the belief that it is in the course of ultimate extinction; or its advocates will push it forward, till it shall become alike lawful in all the States, old as well as new – North as well as South.

Have we no tendency to the latter condition?

Let any one who doubts, carefully contemplate that now almost complete legal combination – piece of machinery so to speak – compounded of the Nebraska doctrine, and the Dred Scott decision. Let him consider not only what work the machinery is adapted to do, and how well adapted; but also, let him study the history of its construction, and trace, if he can, or rather fail, if he can, to trace the evidence of design and concert of action, among its chief architects, from the beginning."

president on June 16, 1858, making his famous "House Divided" speech soon after. In it he stated that the divisions in the United States threatened to tear the Union apart, and that it simply could not survive being "half-slave and half-free." He accepted that slavery was spreading and pledged to reverse the trend.

In the middle of the electioneering, news came that John Brown and his followers had mounted an attack on the Federal arsenal at Harper's Ferry, Virginia, on October 16, 1859. Brown's plan was incredible: with just 13 white men and five black supporters he intended to seize the weapons in the arsenal and set up a fortified base, with himself as leader of a new provisional government. With this established, he would force emancipation. Colonel Robert E. Lee swiftly and effectively dealt with the raid. The two-day siege claimed the lives of two of Brown's sons and eight others and government losses were seven killed. Brown was arrested, tried and hanged on December 2, 1859. He would be immortalized in song, but as the *Richmond Inquirer* prophetically noted: "The Harper's Ferry invasion has advanced the cause of disunion more than any other event that has happened since the formation of the government."

The election campaign pressed on, with four candidates vying for the presidential votes. John Bell of Tennessee stood as the Constitutional Unionist candidate, John C. Breckinridge for the breakaway Southern Democrats, while Lincoln faced the Democrat, Stephen A. Douglas.

By early fall it was clear that the Republicans were winning the hearts of the voters. Election night was November 6, 1860 and Lincoln stormed ahead in an unassailable lead,

snatching all the key Northern states. He received 180 electoral votes, a majority of 37. Douglas won just 12, Breckinridge 72 (all the slave states), and Bell 39.

Lincoln had received only 39.9 percent of the popular vote, while together the Democrats had achieved 47 percent and Bell 14. Had Breckinridge and Douglas run together, however, Lincoln would still have won 169 electoral votes, giving him a majority of 35.

The South had mixed feelings where Lincoln's victory was concerned, even though he came from a slave state

OPPOSITE: Robert E. Lee. General for the Confederacy.

RIGHT: John Bell, Secretary of War from 1841.

LEFT: Exterior Vew of Fort Sumter, Charleston, South Carolina
A Confederate flag flies as the fort explodes. Watercolor by A. Vizitelly, 1863.

and had strong links with the South. The strongest reaction came from South Carolina, which supported the right of the states to secede. In November it decided to call its election delegates to a meeting, and special convention elections would also take place in Alabama, Mississippi, Florida, Georgia, and Louisiana. It was clear that secession was in the air, yet Lincoln had not even been inaugurated; Buchanan still held that

post of president until it was handed over in March 1861.

On December 3, 1860 Buchanan, in his last annual message to Congress, had tried to diffuse the situation. He called on the people to see that the Southerners should be "let alone and permitted to manage their domestic institutions in their own way." He said this in the hope of allying the fears of the South, but added that he saw secession as illegal, in that "such a

ABOVE: The interior of Fort Sumter, Charleston, South Carolina. James Island is in the distance.

OPPOSITE: Fort Moultrie, Charleston, South Carolina.

OVERLEAF: Fort Moultrie, Charleston, South Carolina
Watercolor by A. Vizitelly, 1861.

principle is wholly inconsistent with the history as well as the character of the Federal Constitution." Sitting firmly on the fence, he went on to say that the government did not have the right to prevent a state from leaving the Union: "The power to make war against a state is at variance with the whole spirit and intentions of the Constitution. The fact is our Union rests upon public opinion, and can never be cemented by the blood of its citizens shed in a civil war." Blood would be shed, oceans of it. Buchanan's speech brought solace

OPPOSITE: Interior of Fort Moultrie on Sullivan's Island.

ABOVE: Sheet music for Major Anderson's Grand March.
Major Robert Anderson was in command of Fort Sumter at the beginning of the Civil War.

RIGHT: The Confederate General Joseph E. Johnston.

neither to the South nor the North; in fact it was a matter of concern to them both.

The House of Representatives rapidly created a Committee of Thirty-Three, one person representing each state, while Vice President Breckinridge created the Council of Thirteen in the Senate. The key objective of both committees was to douse the flames of secession and find yet another compromise that both sides could accept as palatable. On the very day that the Council of Thirteen was appointed (December 20), the South Carolina convention adopted an Ordnance of Secession, passed with a vote of 169 to nought. South Carolina published *A Declaration of the Immediate Causes of Secession*, along with an *Address to the Slaveholding States* (written by R. Barnwell Rhett). This action brought three Federal fortifications in the Charleston area into the national spotlight, the first being Castle Pinckney (close to Charleston), the second Fort Moultrie (on Sullivan's Island) and the unfinished Fort Sumter.

The Federal government, wary of the possibilities of secession, had begged for reinforcements to be sent to the area. Now South Carolina was demanding the surrender of the forts. Major Robert Anderson, who was in command of the forts, moved his forces to the one that was more defendable, Sumter, on the basis that it was the hardest to attack.

On January 9, 1861 Mississippi voted to secede, with a vote of 84 to 15, and Florida followed suit the following day, voting 62 to 7 in favor of secession. Alabama was next on January 11, with a pro-secession vote of 61 to 39.

Meanwhile, the Council of Thirteen was still hard at work, desperately seeking to avert disaster. John J. Crittenden proposed a compromise plan to save the Union, but in the end the committee rejected his proposal by seven votes to six. By December 28 the committee was clear

Research Projects

The Fugitive Slave Act of 1850 was passed in Congress as a compromise between the North and the South. Summarize the background to the act and the effects it had on attitudes in the North and South.

that no reconciliation plan could be agreed. Crittenden made more proposals to the senate in early January, three of which the Council of Thirteen accepted: the proper enforcement of the Fugitive Slave Law; an amendment to the U.S. Constitution, stating there would be no interference with slavery where it already existed; and the right of fugitive slaves to a trial by jury.

Several of President Buchanan's cabinet members resigned in late December as their states seceded from the Union. Unionists from the North replaced them, the most significant being the new Attorney General, Edwin M. Stanton. Stanton took a

OPPOSITE LEFT: The Confederate President Jefferson Davis.

OPPOSITE RIGHT: John Jordan Crittenden, (1787–1863) was a politician from Kentucky. He represented the state in both the U.S. House of Representatives and the U.S. Senate and twice served as United States Attorney General.

RIGHT: Castle Pinckney was a small masonry fortification constructed by the U.S. government by 1810 in the harbor of Charleston, South Carolina. It was used very briefly as a prisoner-of-war camp (six weeks) and artillery position during the Civil War.

firm line against the secessionists from the start and would be invaluable to Lincoln in later years.

Attempts were made to reinforce the beleaguered Major Anderson and his men at Fort Sumter, but it was a poorly kept secret. A civilian-chartered paddle steamer, with Union troops on board, the *Star of the West*, came under heavy fire from South Carolina artillery as it attempted to reach the fort. After it had been hit twice, the paddle steamer turned back.

A week later, on January 16, 1861, the Georgia secession convention got underway, passing the Ordnance of Seccession by 208 votes to 89. Four days later the Louisiana convention met at Baton Rouge, and despite attempts to delay the decision, secession was agreed by 113 to 17.

The last state of the Deep South to secede was Texas. Governor Sam Houston was all for the state remaining in the Union and did his best to avert the assembly of a convention. It took place, nevertheless, in Austin on January 28, 1861, the inevitable result being 166 votes to eight in favor of secession.

On February 4, 1861, a Peace Convention assembled in Washington with hopes of reversing the secession decisions and reaching a compromise to save the Union. On the same day, delegates from the seceded states met in Montgomery, Alabama, to create the Confederate States of America. By February 8 they had drafted a new constitution and selected Jefferson Davis of Mississippi as the first provisional president of the Confederacy. Alexander H. Stephens became the vice president, taking the oath of office three days later. Shortly afterwards, Davis formally became president and he made his inaugural address, in which he stated: 'We have changed the constituent parts, but not the system of our government. The Constitution formed by our fathers is that of these Confederate states.'

The Peace Convention finally made seven compromise proposals on February 27, but it was too little too late and what remained was to see how Abraham Lincoln would react, once he became president of what remained of the United States.

On paper, if there was to be war, the vast imbalance between North and South should have made the result a foregone conclusion. The 23 states loyal to the Union (including Kansas) had a population of 22 million, while in the 11 Confederate states, the white population numbered 5.5 million, with a further 3.5 million slaves. Only 9,000

of the 30,000 miles (48300km) of railroad track lay within the South, while 75 per cent of the nation's factories were in the North, together with the vast majority of shipyards and overwhelming proportions of coal and iron.

Virginia finally voted for secession on April 17, closely followed by Arkansas, North Carolina and Tennessee. Importantly, however, Delaware, Maryland, Kentucky and Missouri, all slave states, remained loyal to the Union, though many inhabitants of these four border states did travel south and joined the Confederate forces.

The population and materials imbalance was in part offset by the quality of the Southern rank and file and of its officers. Southern men could ride and shoot, and Southern gentlemen were accustomed to commanding men.

Around 30 percent of the regular Union army officer corps joined the Confederacy, including two men who would become icons of the Confederate armies, Robert E. Lee and Thomas "Stonewall" Jackson. The regular army, rank and file, remained largely loyal, but was a drop in the ocean and only numbered some 16,000 men.

OPPOSITE ABOVE: The Federal Major General Robert Patterson.

OPPOSITE BELOW: Thomas Jonathan "Stonewall" Jackson on his Horse, Little Sorrel
Painting by David Bendann ca. 1913.

RIGHT: The Federal General George Brinton McClellan.

3 he called up 40,034 men to provide the regular army with 22,714 more men and the rest were allocated to the navy.

Meanwhile, on April 16, the Confederate government passed a motion to introduce the conscription of all white men between the ages of 18 and 35 years.

It soon became clear to Lincoln that he would need considerable numbers of men and a great deal of money to bring a swift end to the war. He asked for 400,000 men and $400m. These vast numbers were for the future; what was more pressing was that Washington was just over the Potomac river from Confederate Virginia, and to defend it he would need to rely on only 30,000 or so men, commanded by General Irvin McDowell.

It was an army in name only, in that it was a ragbag of volunteer regiments, mainly former militiamen. Very few of them had ever fired at anything other than a target and were complete novices where drill or battlefield maneuvers were concerned.

In April 1861 a North Carolina newspaper identified the key differences between the armies of the North and South: "The army of the South will be composed of the best material that ever made up an army; whilst that of Lincoln will be gathered from the sewers of the cities – the degraded, beastly off-scourings of all quarters of the world, who will serve for pay, and run away when danger threatens them." This was very close to the mark, as the North would soon discover.

Lincoln was finally inaugurated president on March 4, 1861 and, unlike the hesitant Buchanan, resolved to deal with the secession crisis. Lincoln insisted he had no desire to interfere with slavery but that he would execute the law in all the states. He considered the Union to be unbroken. He would order the holding, occupying, and possession of government property. This clearly referred to Fort Sumter, still holding out in Charleston harbor. Lincoln ordered supplies to be taken to the fort, but before they arrived by ship, the Confederate guns had opened up on the fort. It was April 12 and the next day, with no ammunition left, Fort Sumter surrendered.

On April 15 Lincoln issued the order to muster 75,000 militia with a length of service of 90 days. On May

LEFT: The Confederate General Pierre G.T. Beauregard.

OPPOSITE: Photograph shows participants and crowd at the first inauguration of President Abraham Lincoln, at the U.S. Capitol, Washington, D.C. Lincoln is standing under the wood canopy, at the front, midway between the left and center posts. His face is in shadow but the white shirt front is visible.

OVERLEAF: Manassas National Battlefield Park, Virginia.

The opposing armies faced off with Confederate General Pierre G.T. Beauregard at Manassas Junction, with 20,000 men. General George B. McClellan had a Union army of 20,000 in Virginia and a further 13,000 based at Harper's Ferry under General Patterson. Facing Patterson was General Joseph E. Johnston's force of 10,000 Confederates.

Lincoln ordered McDowell's 30,000 to advance, while Patterson would check Johnston. Lincoln figured that McDowell's army would be more than sufficient to deal with Beauregard's 20,000 men.

It seemed like peacetime maneuvers as McDowell's men began to close on Manassas Junction on July 20, 1861. The next day McDowell ordered his leading units to cross a small stream known as Bull Run.

Text-Dependent Questions

1. When did President Buchanan come to power?

2. What was the Dred Scott case?

3. Who was Robert Edward Lee?

TIME LINE OF THE CIVIL WAR

1860

November 6
Abraham Lincoln elected president.

December 20
South Carolina secedes from the Union, followed two months later by other states.

1861

February 9
Jefferson Davis becomes the first and only President of the Confederate States of America.

March 4
Lincoln sworn in as 16th President of the United States.

April 12
Confederates, under Beauregard, open fire on Fort Sumter at Charleston, South Carolina.

April 15
Lincoln issues a proclamation calling for 75,000 volunteers.

April 17
Virginia secedes from the Union, followed by three other states, making an 11-state Confederacy.

April 19
Blockade proclamation issued by Lincoln.

April 20
Robert E. Lee resigns his command in the United States Army.

July 4
Congress authorizes a call for half a million volunteers.

July 21
Union forces, under McDowell, defeated at Bull Run.

July 27
McClellan replaces McDowell.

November 1
McClellan becomes general-in-chief of Union forces after the resignation of Winfield Scott.

November 8
Two Confederate officials are seized en route to Great Britain by the Union navy.

1862

February 6
Grant captures Fort Henry in Tennessee.

March 8–9
The Confederate ironclad *Merrimac* sinks two Union warships, then fights the *Monitor*.

April 6–7
Confederates attack Grant at Shiloh on the Tennessee river.

April 24
Union ships under Farragut take New Orleans.

May 31
Battle of Seven Pines, where Joseph E. Johnston is badly wounded when he nearly defeats McClellan's army.

June 1
Robert E. Lee takes over from Johnston and renames the force the Army of Northern Virginia.

June 25–July 1
Lee attacks McClellan near Richmond during the Seven Days' Battles. McClellan retreats towards Washington.

July 11
Henry Halleck becomes general -in-chief of the Union army.

August 29–30
Union army, under Pope, defeated by Jackson and Longstreet at the Second Battle of Bull Run.

September 4–9
Lee invades the North, pursued by McClellan's Union army.

September 17
Battle of Antietam. Both sides are badly mauled. Lee withdraws to Virginia.

September 22
Preliminary Emancipation Proclamation issued by Lincoln.

November 7
McClellan replaced by Burnside as commander of the Army of the Potomac.

December 13
Burnside decisively defeated at Fredericksburg, Virginia, 1863.

1863
January 1
Lincoln issues the final Emancipation Proclamation.

January 29
Grant assumes command of the Army of the West.

March 3
U.S. Congress authorizes conscription.

May 1–4
Hooker is decisively defeated by Lee at the Battle of Chancellorsville. Stonewall Jackson is mortally wounded.

June 3
Lee invades the North, heading into Pennsylvania.

June 28
George Meade replaces Hooker as commander of the Army of the Potomac.

July 1–3
Lee is defeated at the Battle of Gettysburg.

July 4
Vicksburg – the last Confederate stronghold on the Mississippi – falls to Grant and the Confederacy is now split in two.

July 13–16
Draft riots in New York

July 18
54th Massachusetts, under Shaw, fails in its assault against Fort Wagner, South Carolina.

August 21
Quantrill's raiders murder the inhabitants of Lawrence, Kansas

September 19–20
Bragg's Confederate Army of Tennessee defeats General Rosecrans at Chickamauga.

October 16
Grant given command of all operations in the West.

November 19
Lincoln gives his famous Gettysburg Address.

November 23–25
Grant defeats Bragg at Chattanooga.

1864
March 9
Grant assumes command of all armies of the Union. Sherman takes Grant's old job as commander in the West.

May 5–6
Battle of the Wilderness.

May 8–12
Battle of Spotsylvania.

Slavery and the Abolition Movement

June 1–3
Battle of Cold Harbor.

June 15
Union troops miss a chance to capture Petersburg.

July 20
Sherman defeats Hood at Atlanta.

August 29
Former General McClellan becomes the Democratic nominee for president.

September 2
Atlanta is captured by Sherman.

October 19
Sheridan defeats Early's Confederates in the Shenandoah Valley.

November 8
Lincoln is re-elected president.

November 15
Sherman begins his March to the Sea.

December 15–16
Hood is defeated at the Battle of Nashville.

December 21 Sherman reached Savannah in Georgia.

1865
January 31
Thirteenth amendment approved to abolish slavery.

February 3
Peace conference between Lincoln and Confederate vice president fails at Hampton Roads, Virginia.

March 4
Lincoln inaugurated as president.

March 25
Lee's last offensive is defeated after four hours at Petersburg.

April 2
Grant pushes through Lee's defensive lines at Petersburg. Richmond is evacuated as Union troops enter.

April 4
Lincoln tours Richmond.

April 9
Lee surrenders his army to Grant at Appomattox Courthouse, Virginia.

April 10
Major victory celebrations in Washington.

April 14
Lincoln shot in a Washington theater.

April 15
Lincoln dies and Andrew Johnson becomes president.

April 18
Confederate General Johnston surrenders to Sherman in North Carolina.

April 19
Lincoln's funeral procession.

April 26
Lincoln's assassin, Booth, is shot and dies in Virginia.

May 23–24
Victory parade held in Washington.

December 6
Thirteenth Amendment approved by Congress. It is ratified and slavery is formally abolished.

BELOW: Civil War Cemetery at Stones River National Battlefield, Rutherford County, Tennessee.

Educational Videos about the American Civil War

The Gettysburg Address
A speech by U.S. President Abraham Lincoln, one of the best-known in American history. It was delivered by Lincoln during the American Civil War, on the afternoon of Thursday, November 19, 1863, at the dedication of the Soldiers' National Cemetery in Gettysburg, Pennsylvania.

Everyday Animated Map
A useful video explaining how the Union and Confederate armies gained ground through the various battles.

"Dear Sarah," A Soldier's Farewell to his Wife
A Civil War soldier's heartbreaking farewell letter written before his death at Bull Run.

The War Between the States
Historian Garry Adleman gives an overview of the causes, campaigns, and conclusion of the Civil War.

History, Key Figures, and Battles
A useful, concise dramatized, video explaining the American Civil War.

EXAMPLES OF CONFEDERATE UNIFORMS

Robert E. Lee in his general's uniform

Trooper, Stuart's Cavalry Corps.

Infantry Soldier

Marines

Virginia Cavalry

Louisiana
Tigers

Georgia
Infantry

4th Alabama
Regiment

South
Carolina
Regiment

Engineer

EXAMPLES OF UNION (FEDERAL) UNIFORMS

Ulysses S. Grant in his general's uniform

Indiana Regiment

5th New York Volunteers

39th New York Voluntry Infantry Regiment

Iron Brigade of the U.S.

U.S. Marine Corps

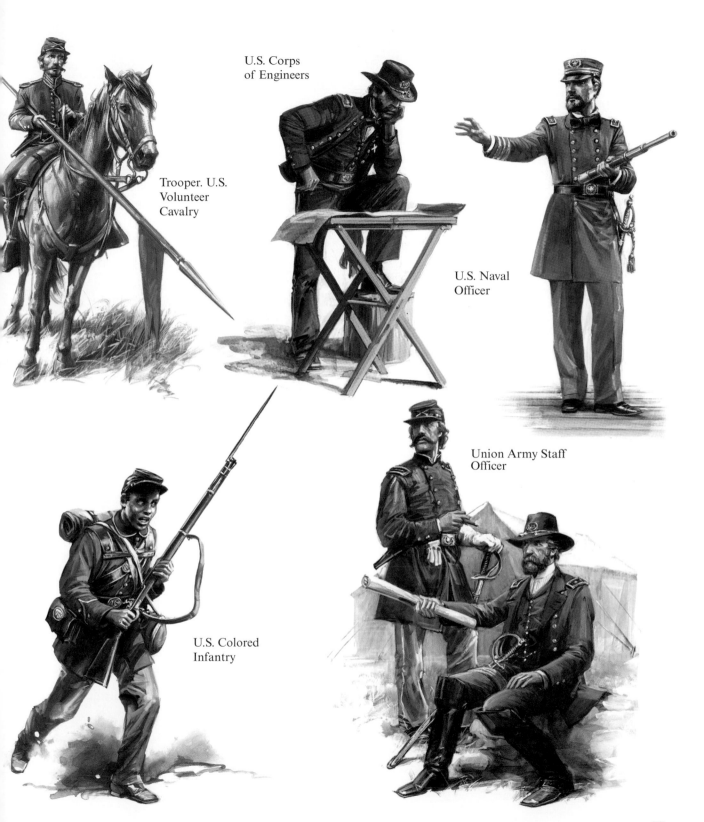

Trooper. U.S. Volunteer Cavalry

U.S. Corps of Engineers

U.S. Naval Officer

Union Army Staff Officer

U.S. Colored Infantry

Series Glossary of Key Terms

Abolitionist A person who wants to eliminate slavery.

Antebellum A term describing the United States before the Civil War.

Artillery Large bore firearms like cannons and mortars.

Assassination A murder for political reasons (usually an important person).

Cash Crop A crop such as cotton, sugar cane, or tobacco sold for cash.

Cavalry A section of the military mounted on horseback.

Confederacy Also called the South or the Confederate States of America. A term given to 11 southern states seceding from the United States in 1860 and 1861.

Copperhead A person in the North who sympathized with the South during the Civil war.

Dixie A nickname given to states in the south-east United States.

Dred Scott Decision A decision made by the Supreme Court that said Congress could not outlaw slavery.

Emancipation An act of setting someone free from slavery.

Gabion A basket filled with rocks and earth used to build fortifications.

Fugitive Slave Law A law passed by Congress in 1850 that stipulated escaped slaves in free states had to be retured to their owners.

Infantry Soldiers that travel and fight on foot.

North The states located in the north of the United States, also called the Union.

Plantation An area of land especially in hot parts of the world where crops such as cotton and tobacco are grown.

Slavery The state of a person who is owned or under the control of another.

Secession Withdrawal from the Federal goverment of the United States.

Sectionalism A tendency to be concerned with local interests and customs ahead of the larger country.

South The states located in the south of the United States, also called the Confederacy.

Union The name given to the states that stayed loyal to the United States.

West Point The United States Military Academy.

Yankee A nickname given for people from the North and Union soldiers.

Further Reading and Internet Resources

WEBSITES

http://www.civilwar.org

http://www.historyplace.com/civilwar

http://www.historynet.com/civil-war

www.britannica.com/event/American-Civil-War

BOOKS

Bruce Catton. *The Centennial History of the Civil War,* Doubleday, 1962. Kindle edition 2013.

Ulysses S. Grant. *The Complete Personal Memoirs of Ulysses S.* Grant Seven Treasures Publications, 2009

James Robertson and Neil Kagan. *The Untold Civil War: Exploring the Human Side of War.* National Geographic, 2011.

If you enjoyed this book take a look at Mason Crest's other war series:

The Vietnam War, World War II, Major U.S. Historical Wars.

Index

In this book, page numbers in **bold italic font** indicate photos or videos.

A

"The Abolition Catastrophe," *20*
abolitionist groups, 35–36
  See also American Anti-Slavery Society; American Colonization Society
abolitionist movement, 19, 20, 22, 30–31, 35
abolitionists, 25
  See also Douglass, Frederick; Garrison, William Lloyd; Lundy, Benjamin; Quakers; Tubman, Harriet
"Abolition of the Slave Trade or The Man, the Master," *23*
Abraham Lincoln (Healy), *49*
Adams, John Quincy, 22, *22*, 31
Address to the Slaveholding States, 60
African Americans, *2*, *3*
  See also "Distinguished Colored Men"; slaves
African Methodist Episcopal Church, 25
Allen, Richard, *24*, 25
American Anti-Slavery Society, 27–29
American Colonization Society, 18, 22–23, 25, 26
"Am I Not a Man and a Brother?," *22*
Anderson, Robert, 59, 61, 62
anti-slavery movement. *See* abolitionist movement
Army of the Potomac, *2*
Atlanta, Ga., *15*

A

Baptists, 30
Barnard, George, 14
Basset, E.D., *24*
Beauregard, Pierre G. T., 64–65, *64*
Beecher, Henry Ward, *18*
Bell, John, 51, *51*
Birney, James, 25, *25*, *34*, 35–36
black abolitionist group, 36
  See also Douglass, Frederick
Breckinridge, John C., *48*, 51, 60
Brown, Henry Box, *28*
Brown, John, 21, 39, *39*, *40–41*, 47, 51
Brown, William Wells, *24*
Bruce, Blanche K., *24*
Buchanan, James, *46*, 47–48, 54, 59
The burning of the U.S. Arsenal at

Harper's Ferry, April 18, 1861 (Strother), *42*

C

Canada, 23
cartoons, *20*
Castle Pinckney, Charleston, S.C., 60, 61, *61*
Celebration of the Abolition of Slavery in the District of Columbia by the Colored People, Washington, April, 19 1866 (Dielman), *31*
cemeteries, *70*
church rifts, 30
Civil War timeline, 68–70
Clay, Henry, *38*, 43
Coffin, Livi, 25
colonization, 26
  See also American Colonization Society
Combahee Ferry, S.C., raid, 21
Committee of Thirty-Three, 60
Confederate army, 63–64, 65
Confederate States of America, 62
Confederate uniforms, *72–73*
conscription, 64
Convention for Promoting the Abolition of Slavery, 26
cotton gin, *14*
cotton plantation, *16–17*
Council of Thirteen, 60, 61
Crandall, Prudence, 30, *30*
Crittenden, John Jordan, 60, 61

D

Davis, Jefferson, *60*, 62
Declaration of Independence, 18–19
A Declaration of the Immediate Causes of Secession, 60
"Distinguished Colored Men," *24*
Douglas, Stephen A., 47, *47*, 51
Douglass, Frederick, *24*, *26*, 27, *27*, *28*, 36
Dred Scott case, *39*, 48

E

Ecclesiasticals, 35
  See also Methodists
Elijah Parish Lovejoy Was Killed By a Proslavery Mob November 7, 1837, *32–33*
Elliott, Robert Brown, *24*

emancipation, Quakers and, 17
Emancipation Act anniversary celebration, *3*, *31*
Emancipation of the Slaves, *37*
Emancipation Ordinance of Missouri, *36*, 37
emancipation with compensation, 20
emancipation without compensation, 28
Exterior Vew of Fort Sumter, Charleston, S.C. (Vizitelly), *52–53*

F

Fort Moultrie, Charleston, S.C., *55*, *58*, 60–61
Fort Moultrie, Charleston, S.C. (Vizitelly), *56–57*
Fort Sumter, S.C., *52–53*, *54*, 59, 61, 62, 64
freed slaves, *12–13*, 20
Fugitive Slave Act, 23, 39, 43
"The Fugitive's Song" lithograph, *26*

G

gag rule, 31, 35
Garnet, Henry Highland, *24*
Garrett, Thomas, 25
Garrison, William Lloyd, 14, 18, *18*, 26–27, 30, 35
The Genius of Universal Emancipation, 26
George, General, *63*
George III, 18
"Get off the Track!" (Hutchinson), *19*
Giddings, Joshua R., 29, *29*, 37
Grant, Ulysses S., *74*
Greeley, Horace, *18*
Greener, R.T., *24*

H

Harper's Ferry, W.Va., *44–45*
Harper's Ferry Arsenal invasion and ruins, 21, *40–41*, *42*, *43*, 51
Hopper, Isaac, 25
"House Divided" speech (Lincoln), 49
Houston, Sam, 62
Hutchinson, Jesse, Jr., 19

J

Jackson, Thomas "Stonewall," *62*, 63
Jefferson, Thomas, 18, 20
J.J. Smith plantation, Beaufort, S.C., *5*, *12–13*
Johnston, Joseph E., *59*, 65

K
Kansas, 47
Knapp, Isaac, 14

L
Langston, John Mercer, *24*
Lee, Robert E., *50*, 51, 63, *72*
Letters on Slavery (Rankin), 18
The Liberator, 14, 25
Liberia, 23
Liberty Party, 35–36
Lincoln, Abraham
    "The Abolition Catastrophe," 20, *20*
    about, *8*, *49*
    election campaign, 48–49, 51
    Emancipation of the Slaves, *37*
    inauguration of, *65*
    post-inauguration actions, 64
    Union army and, 65
Lovejoy, Elijah Parish, 33, 35
Lundy, Benjamin, 25–26

M
"Major Anderson's March,' *59*
Manassas National Battlefield Park, Va.,
    66–67
McClellan, George B., 20, *20*, 65
McDowell, Irvin, 64
Methodists, 17, 30

N
Negro Convention Movement, 25
New England Anti-Slavery Society, 27
the North
    abolitionist movement in, 19
    Fugitive Slave Act and, 39, 43
    See also abolitionist groups;
      abolitionists
North-West Ordnance, 20

O
Old State Capitol, Springfield, Ill., *49*
Ordnance of Secession, 60, 62

P
"The Parting – Buy Us Too," *19*
Patterson, Robert, *62*, 65
Peace Convention, 62
petition system, 29, 31
Philanthropist, 35
Phillips, Wendell, *18*
Pinchback, P.B.S., *24*

"Pioneers of Freedom," *18*
plantations, *5*, *12–13*, *16–17*, *35*
political abolitionists, 35–36
    See also Birney, James
population, Union versus Confederate
    states, 62
Presbyterians, 17, 30
pro-slavery lobby, 43, 47

Q
Quakers, 17, 25

R
radical abolitionists, 35, 36–37
    See also Garrison, William Lloyd;
      Giddings, Joshua R.; Lincoln,
      Abraham; Phillips, Wendell
railroad lines, 62–63
Rainey, J.H., *24*
Rankin, John, 18, 23
reward for capture, 30
Rice, David, 17–18
Richmond Inquirer, 51
riots, 35
Rogers, Nathanial Peabody, 19
runaway slaves, 21, 23
    See also Underground Railroad
The Saint Louis Observer, 33

S
Scott, Dred, *38*, 39, *39*, 48
Scott, Orange, 35
secession, 54, 59–60, 61, 62, 63
Shadrach, 43
slave auction block, Green Hill
    Plantation, Va., *35*
slave being separated from family
    (Stephens), *19*
slave being sold (Stephens), *18*
slave owners, 22, 26–27
Slavery Inconsistent with Justice and
    Good Policy (Rice), 17
slaves, *5*, *12–13*, *14*, 19
    See also freed slaves; Scott, Dred
slave trade, end of, 39
slave trader, Alexandria, Va., *6*
Smith, Gerrit, *18*
Smith plantation. *See* J.J. Smith
    plantation, Beaufort, S.C.
Society for the Abolition of Slavery in
    England seal, *22*
soldiers eating, *2*

Some Considerations on the Keeping of
    Negroes (Woolman), 17
the South, 30–31, 35, 43, 47, 51, 54
South Carolina
    Castle Pinckney, Charleston, 60, 61,
      61
    Combahee Ferry raid, 21
    Fort Moultrie, Charleston, *55*, *56–57*,
      58, 60–61
    Fort Sumter, *52–53*, *54*, 59, 61, 62,
      64
    J.J. Smith plantation, Beaufort, *5*,
      12–13
    secession and, 60
Stanton, Edwin M., 61–62
Star of the West, 62
Stephens, Alexander H., 62
Stones River National Battlefield
    cemetery, Tenn., *70*
Sumner, Charles, *18*

T
Tappan, Arthur, *26*, 27, 30
Tappan, Lewis, 27
Thomas Jonathan "Stonewall" Jackson
    on his Horse, Little Sorrel (Bendann),
    62
Thoughts on African Colonization
    (Garrison), 26
Tubman, Harriet, 21, *21*, 25

U
Underground Railroad, 21, 23, 25
Union army, 21, 63–64, 65
Union army guard, *6*
Union uniforms, *74–75*
Union versus Confederate states
    imbalances, 62–63

W
Wedgwood, Josiah, 22
Western territories, 20, 37, 38
Wilson, Henry, *18*
Woolman, John, 17

PHOTOGRAPHIC ACKNOWLEDGEMENTS

All images in this book are supplied by the Library of Congess/public domain and under license from © Shutterstock.com other than the following: Regency House Publishing Limited: 7, 72-73, 74-75.

The content of this book was first published as *CIVIL WAR*.

ABOUT THE AUTHOR

Johnathan Sutherland & Diane Canwell

Together, Diane Canwell and Jonathan Sutherland are the authors of 150 books, and have written extensively about the American Civil War. Both have a particular interest in American history, and its military aspects in particular. Several of their books have attracted prizes and awards, including New York Library's Best of Reference and Book List's Editor's Choice.